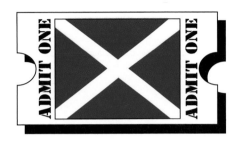

FACES
AND
PLACES

SCOTLAND

BY MARYCATE O'SULLIVAN

THE CHILD'S WORLD®, INC.

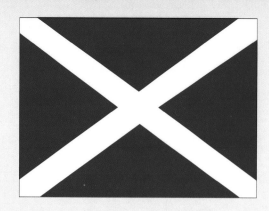

COVER PHOTO

A member of the Saint Andrews Girls' Brigade.
©Dave Bartruff/CORBIS

Published in the United States of America by The Child's World®, Inc.
PO Box 326
Chanhassen, MN 55317-0326
800-599-READ
www.childsworld.com

Project Manager James R. Rothaus/James R. Rothaus & Associates
Designer Robert E. Bonaker/R. E. Bonaker & Associates
Contributors Mary Berendes, Katherine Stevenson, Ph.D., Red Line Editorial

Library of Congress Cataloging-in-Publication Data
O'Sullivan, MaryCate, 1973-
Scotland / by MaryCate O'Sullivan.
p. cm.
Includes index.
ISBN 1-56766-909-3 (lib. bdg. : alk. paper)
1. Scotland—Juvenile Literature.
[1. Scotland]
I. Title.
DA762 .O88 2001
941.1—dc21

Table of Contents

If you could look at Earth from the Moon, you would see large areas of water, ice, and land. The large land areas are called **continents**. Next to the continent of Europe lies the island of Great Britain. Great Britain includes Scotland in the north and England and Wales in the south.

Western Hemisphere

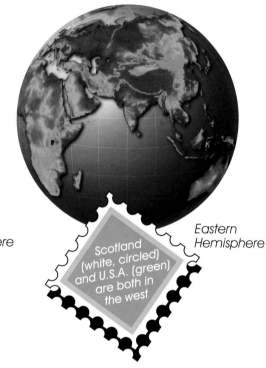

Eastern Hemisphere

Scotland (white, circled) and U.S.A. (green) are both in the west

England, Scotland, and Wales, together with nearby Northern Ireland, make up a nation called the United Kingdom.

Scotland is surrounded on three sides by water. To the north and west is the Atlantic Ocean. To the east is the North Sea.

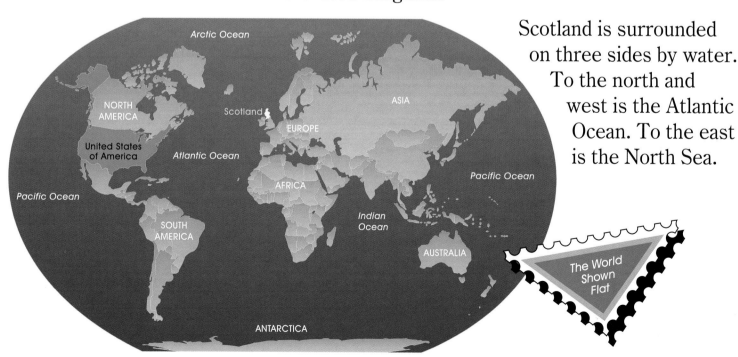

The World Shown Flat

Atlantic Ocean

North Sea

SCOTLAND
(UNITED KINGDOM)

NORTHERN
IRELAND
(UNITED KINGDOM)

ISLAND OF
GREAT BRITAIN

Irish Sea

IRELAND

WALES
(UNITED
KINGDOM)

ENGLAND
(UNITED KINGDOM)

Close-Up
of
Scotland

The Slopes
And Valleys
Of Glen Lyon

SHETLAND ISLANDS

ORKNEY ISLANDS

HEBRIDES ISLANDS

Rannoch • • Glen Lyon

★ Edinburgh

The Blackmount Mountains Seen From Rannoch Moor

Scotland has three main areas of land: the Highlands, the Central Lowlands, and the Southern Uplands. The rocky Highlands cover much of the country. These mountainous areas have steep slopes separated by narrow valleys called *glens*. The Central Lowlands area has low hills and broad fields.

The Southern Uplands region has taller hills, rocky cliffs, and boggy, treeless areas called **moors**.

Scotland's coastline is rugged and scenic. Some of the coastal areas have wide bays called *firths*. Inland from the coast there are beautiful lakes called *lochs* (LOKS). Scotland also has small islands offshore. The Hebrides (HEB-rih-deez) Islands lie to the west. The Orkney and Shetland Islands lie to the north.

Olna Firth On The Shetland Islands

Heather Growing On A Hill In Keith

©Macduff Everton/CORBIS

Because so much of Scotland is rocky and steep, few types of plants and trees grow there. Only about 15% of Scotland is forested. Oak and birch trees grow in small forests scattered across the countryside. In the Highlands and Southern Uplands, low grasses are common. A green bush called **heather** turns the hills purple when its colorful flowers appear.

Wild Shetland Ponies On Foula

©Kevin Schafer/CORBIS

Much of Scotland's animal life lives in the Highlands and on the islands. Larger animals, such as red deer and Highland cattle, are found in the Highlands. Small, thick-coated Shetland ponies live on the Shetland Islands. Birds such as golden eagles and kestrels soar high above Scotland's mountains. Many types of fish, such as salmon and trout, live in the lochs and rivers along the coasts.

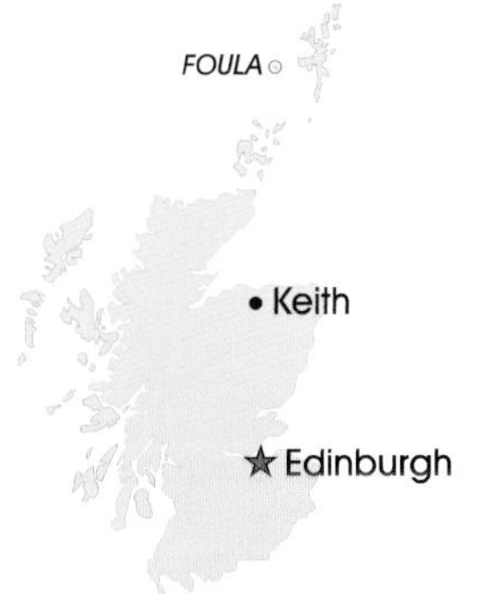

FOULA ⊙

• Keith

★ Edinburgh

Greylag
Geese In
Edinburgh

Ruins Of Celtic Stone-Built Houses On The Hillside Near Kelhead

Galloway • • Kelhead

©Papillio/CORBIS

Ruins Of
Caerlaverock
Castle In
Galloway

©Franz-Marc Frei/CORBIS

People have been living in Scotland for more than 7,000 years. Scientists think that Scotland's first people were hunters and fishermen who came to the area by boat. Over time, more people came to Scotland and settled farther inland. About 3,000 years ago, tribes of Celts (KELTS) began arriving from Europe. The Celts were strong warriors and often battled each other for control of the land.

About 2,000 years ago, the Romans invaded the island of Great Britain.

They took over the southern part (now England) but were unable to conquer the fierce Celts in the north. To keep the Celts in place, the Roman emperor Hadrian built Hadrian's Wall, a huge wall that ran across the whole island. After about 400 years, the Romans left Great Britain, and many people and tribes battled to rule Scotland and England.

Snow
Covering
Hadrian's
Wall

©Adam Woolfitt/CORBIS

Glasgow City Chambers On The River Clyde

©Adam Wolfitt/CORBIS

In 1296, the king of England captured the king of Scotland—and claimed Scotland for his own. The main Celtic tribe, called the Scots, were furious about being under English rule. In 1297, they chased the English back across the border. Years of fighting between Scottish and English groups followed.

A Scottish-English Border Sign Near Berwick On Tweed

After more than 400 years of fighting, peace was finally reached. In 1707, England and Scotland were brought under one government.

Today, Scotland is part of the United Kingdom of Great Britain and Northern Ireland. The prime minister and the queen of England rule over the entire United Kingdom. Laws are made by a **parliament** of elected leaders. But Scotland also has its own laws, courts, and bank systems. Scotland is a very special place—it seems to be a country within a country!

ACROSS THE BORDER

SCOTLAND ✕ ✚ ENGLAND

©Milepost 92¹/²/CORBIS

Glasgow • ★ Edinburgh
• Berwick on Tweed

©Catherine Karnow/CORBIS

ISLE OF LEWIS

• Blair Atholl

• Dunoon

A Highland
Dancer In
Blair Atholl

©Adam Wolfitt/CORBIS

Scotland is home to about 5 million people. Most are relatives of groups that came to the island long ago, such as the Celts. Scottish people are very proud of their **heritage**, and traditional ways of doing things is very important.

One important part of Scotland's heritage is its **clans**, or large groups of related families. Long ago, each clan lived in its own area and had its own chief. Each clan also had its own colorful patterned cloth, or **tartan**. The tartans were used for traditional kinds of clothing, such as pleated **kilts**.

Tweed
Weavers
On The
Isle Of Lewis

©Owen Franken/CORBIS

Scottish people remember their clan histories with pride. Sometimes clans gather in the Highlands for music, dancing, and sporting events—a little like a huge family reunion!

Shepherds Stopping To Talk On A Country Road

©Dewitt Jones/CORBIS

Most of Scotland's people live in cities and towns in the Central Lowlands. Larger cities, such as Glasgow and Edinburgh (ED-'n-bur-uh), are much like those in the United States. They have shops, factories, hotels, banks, and busy streets full of cars and buses. Also like in the United States, city dwellers live in small houses or apartments.

Scottish cities have some beautiful old buildings. In the capital city of Edinburgh, a huge castle stands on top of a high hill. Parts of the castle are over 850 years old!

Homes In Edinburgh

©Adam Woolfitt/CORBIS

In the countryside, away from the busy cities, life is quieter and slower. Most country dwellers live in small towns or villages. They usually live in houses or cottages rather than apartment buildings. Many people who live in the country drive into the larger cities to work each day.

★ Edinburgh

Edinburgh
Castle In
Edinburgh

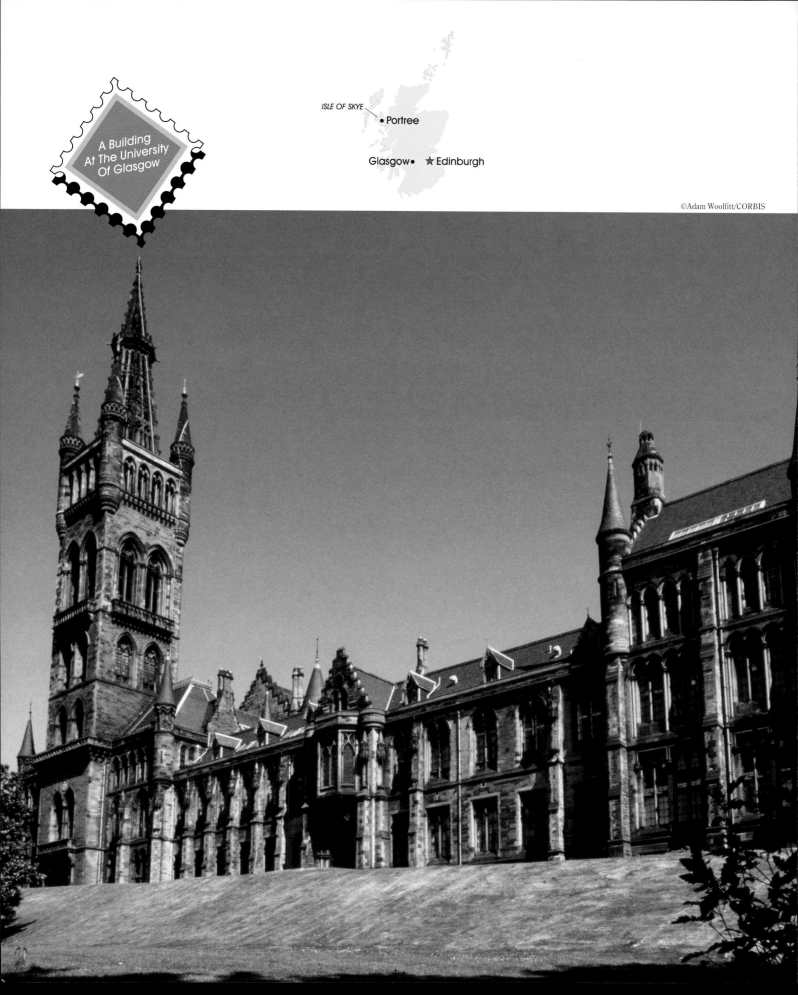

A Building
At The University
Of Glasgow

ISLE OF SKYE • Portree

Glasgow• ★Edinburgh

©Adam Woolfitt/CORBIS

A Man Learning To Play The Bagpipes At The Bagpipe School In Edinburgh

Education is very important in Scotland. Children work hard at school and often begin when they are only 5 years old. Scottish schoolchildren learn subjects such as math, science, and reading, just as you do. Children may leave school when they are 16 years old, but many go on to study at one of Scotland's universities.

English is Scotland's official language. The Gaelic (GAY-lik) language is also spoken in some areas, such as the Highlands and the smaller islands. Gaelic is a very old language that came from the long-ago Celts. A **dialect** of English called *Lallans* is also spoken in many areas of Scotland. Lallans is known for its rolling "r" sounds.

©Adam Woolfitt/CORBIS

TROUT AND SALMON FISHING

PERMITS AVAILABLE HERE

A Fishing Permit Sign In Portree On The Isle Of Skye

A Golf Club Maker In Saint Andrews

Scotland's people work at thousands of different jobs. Some work at banks or other large companies. Others run shops or restaurants. Many work at factories that make things such as electronic equipment, computers, clothes, and whisky.

In Scotland's few farming areas, people grow crops such as potatoes, barley, and wheat. Others raise cattle or sheep. On Scotland's coasts and smaller islands, people catch fish to sell in the markets.

A Shipbuilder In Edinburgh

Many Scottish people work in jobs related to **tourism**—entertaining visitors who come to their country. The visitors want to see this beautiful land and learn about its history. During their visits, they stay in hotels, shop in stores, and eat in restaurants. Providing these services creates many jobs for the Scottish people.

Work

Saint Andrews
★ Edinburgh
• Eyemouth

A Fisherman
Repairing His Nets
In Eyemouth

ISLE OF SKYE

• Blair Atholl

Food

Meat and fish are popular foods in Scotland. Angus beef steaks are favorites, and so is salmon. *Kippers,* or smoked herring, are often eaten for breakfast. Scots also use oatmeal in many recipes, especially for porridge and oatcakes (which are a little like flat pancakes).

The most famous Scottish dish is called *haggis.* To make it, the liver, lungs, and heart of a sheep are chopped up and mixed with oatmeal. Then the mixture is stuffed into a bag made from the sheep's stomach. The bag is then boiled until the meat is cooked.

A Butcher With Haggis On The Isle Of Skye

©Robert Holmes/CORBIS

Kippers And Orange Juice For Breakfast In Blair Atholl

©Macduff Everton/CORBIS

Foods from other countries are also popular in Scotland. Restaurants in larger cities serve Italian, Indian, and even American dishes. Just as in other parts of the United Kingdom, tea is a popular drink.

Scotland's favorite sport is soccer. Also popular is rugby, a rough game a little like American football. Another favorite pastime is golf. In fact, the game of golf began on Scotland's rolling hills. Scotland's famous Highland games, usually held in the spring and summer, are hundreds of years old. Athletes compete in events to show their strength. In "tossing the caber," the athlete throws an enormous wooden pole and tries to flip it over in the air!

Scots celebrate many of the same holidays Americans do, such as Christmas, Easter, and New Year's Day. They also have special holidays of their own, such as Boxing Day (December 26) and Burns Night (January 25). Burns Night celebrates the birthday of famous Scottish poet Robert Burns. At "Burns Suppers," haggis is the featured dish.

Scotland is an ancient land with rocky mountains, deep valleys, and beautiful lakes. It is a place where people proudly remember their past but also look forward to the future. Perhaps someday you will visit Scotland. If you do, think of all these differences— and how they work so well together!

Scotland (White) And France (Blue) Playing Rugby In Edinburgh

© TempSport/CORBIS

ISLE OF SKYE

• Aberdeen

+ BEN NEVIS

• Gleneagles
Renfrew • • ★ Edinburgh
Glasgow

©Hubert S

Area
About 30,400 square miles
(78,800 square kilometers)—a little bigger than South Carolina.

Population
About 5 million people.

Capital City
Edinburgh.

Other Important Cities
Glasgow, Renfrew, and Aberdeen.

Money
The pound sterling, which is divided into 100 pence.

National Language
English. Gaelic is also spoken in some areas.

National Song
Scotland's national song is "God Save the Queen," which is the United
Kingdom's anthem.

National Flag
Officially, Scotland flies the Union Jack—the flag of the United Kingdom.
Unofficially, the traditional Scottish flag is the St. Andrew's Cross. It is a
blue square with two crossed white stripes. The Scottish people have flown
the St. Andrew's Cross for hundreds of years.

Head of Government
The prime minister of Great Britain.

Head of State
The queen of England.

Did You Know?

For years, people have claimed that a monster lives in Scotland's deep Loch Ness. Many say they have seen the creature, and some have pictures of what they think is "Nessie." Scientists are now using special equipment to see whether there really is a creature in the deep lake.

Scotland is famous for its castles and towers—in fact, it has over 600 of them! Some are crumbling ruins, while others, such as Edinburgh Castle, are in fairly good condition.

Scottish poet Robert Burns wrote one of the world's most famous songs, "Auld Lang Syne." The title of this song of friendship means "old long since" or "days of long ago" in the Scottish dialect. Americans often sing it at New Year's parties to celebrate the passing of the old year.

Bagpipes are the most famous Scottish instrument. A set of bagpipes usually has four pipes, a bag, and a tube for blowing air into the bag. After filling the bag with air, the piper squeezes it with one elbow. The squeezed air goes out through three pipes, making different sounds. The piper plays the melody on a fourth pipe.

Ben Nevis, in Scotland's Highlands, is the tallest mountain in Great Britain. It stands 4,406 feet (1,343 meters) high.

How Do You Say?

	SCOTTISH GAELIC	HOW TO SAY IT
Good day	Là math	LAH–mah
How are you?	Ciamar a tha sibh?	KAY–mur ah HAH shiv?
Good-bye	Beannachd leat	bee–AH–nakth LEHT
Thank you	Tapadh leibh	TAH–puh LEEV
One	a h-aon	uh–HUUN
Two	a dhà	uh–GHA
Three	a trì	uh–TREE
Scotland	Alba	ah–LAH–beh

clans (KLANZ)
Clans are large groups of families who are all related to each other. Clans played an important part in Scottish history.

continents (KON-tih-nents)
Earth's continents are large land masses surrounded mostly by water. Scotland is on an island near the continent of Europe.

dialect (DY-uh-lekt)
A dialect is a different form of a language. Lallans is a dialect of English that is spoken in Scotland.

heather (HEH-ther)
Heather is a green shrub that produces purple flowers. Many heather bushes grow in Scotland's Highlands and Southern Uplands.

heritage (HAYR-ih-tej)
Heritage is a person's background, customs, and traditions. The Scottish people are very proud of their heritage.

kilts (KILTS)
Kilts are knee-length pleated skirts traditionally worn by Scottish men.

moors (MOORZ)
Moors are wide, treeless areas usually covered with low grasses and wet bogs. Scotland's Southern Uplands region has many moors.

parliament (PAR-leh-ment)
A parliament is a group of elected leaders who make a nation's laws. The United Kingdom has a parliament.

tartan (TAR-tn)
A tartan is a thick cloth with a colorful pattern of crisscrossed stripes. Each Scottish clan had its own tartan pattern.

tourism (TOOR-ih-zem)
Tourism is the business of entertaining travelers and showing them around a country. Tourism is an important business in Scotland.

Index

Web Sites

Learn more about Scotland:
http://www.britcoun.org/scotland/
http://www.scotland.org/
http://www.discover-scotland.com/
http://www.lonelyplanet.com.au/dest/eur/sco.htm
http://www.scotland.net/

Learn about the legend of the Loch Ness monster:
http://www.pbs.org/wgbh/nova/lochness/legend.html
http://www.lochness.co.uk/

Learn how to say more words in Gaelic:
http://www.smo.uhi.ac.uk/gaidhlig/ionnsachadh/bac/

Listen to Scotland's (the United Kingdom's) national anthem:
http://www.emulateme.com/anthems/unitedkingtexte.htm